Wondering Ardor

Wondering Ardor

by

Tracy Carol Taylor

Wondering Ardor

This is a work of fiction. Names, characters, places, and incidents either are the product of the author's imagination or are used fictitiously, and any resemblance to actual persons, living or dead, businesses establishments, events, or locales is entirely coincidental. The publisher does not have any control over and does not assume any responsibility for author or third-party websites or their contents.

Copyright © 2003 by Prince of Pages, Inc.

All rights reserved.

No part of this book may be reproduced, scanned, or distributed in any printed or electronic form without permission. Please do not participate or encourage piracy of copyrighted materials in violation of the author's rights. Purchase only authorized editions.

Prince of Pages, Inc.

N. Carlin Springs Road.

Arlington, VA 22203

www.princeofpages.com

ISBN: 978-1-9492521-9-4

Cover Art by Getty Images

Contents

Part I. Books

GOTHAM NIGHTS	3
HEARTS OF SNOW	6
SABINA HALL	8
WHAT KIND OF A MAN?	13

Part II. Bi-Lingual

DIVERTIDO	19
NADA ES ME CULPA	20
QUE ES SU PROBLEMA?	23

Part III. Church

EASTER SUNDAY	29

THE GOOD SHEPHERD	33
THE MAN FROM GALILEE	37
MY HEAVENLY FATHER	41
REJOICE	42
SHOW ME THE WAY	46
THANK YOU, JESUS THANK YOU	47
THE TRIAL	49

Part IV. Death

THE COLOR OF DOOM	55
I MISS MY LIFE, MY LOVE	56
SAM'S DAY	58

Part V. Love

FOR THE LOVE OF ROSES	61
MY NEW LOVE	62
ON MY WEDDING DAY	64
QUIET PONDERINGS	67
SQUISHY FEELINGS	69

TEASING THOUGHTS	71
WHAT MIGHT HAVE BEEN	72
WILD ONE	74

Part VI. Persons

CYNTHA J.	77
IAN	78
SAM'S LULLABY	80
STEPHEN M	81
THOMAS L.	82

Part VII. Reflections

BENEATH THE WATERFALL	85
LIKE CHILDREN	87
NIGHT DREAMING	89
TAUGHT TO CARE	90
WHAT WILL THIS DAY BRING?	92

Part VIII. Silly Things

BOTTLES AND CANS	97
CHRISTMAS COUNTING	99
HAPPY ROCK-N-ROLLERS	100
KENTUCKY WINE	102
MICE SLAYERS	104
MY RAT	106
THE OCEAN	107
TAKE YOUR DISHES WITH YOU	108
THAT DAY	110
THE WED OF ROCK AND CLASSICAL	111

Part IX. Television Shows

BLACK VANS AND HELICOPTERS	115
CARMEN SANDIEGO	118
GABRIELLE'S DEFENSE	121
IN THE GALACTIC SPACE FORCE	125

Part X. Work

BORED OUT OF MY MIND	131
GET ME OUT OF THIS TOWN	133
IT'S A QUARTER TILL FIVE	135
ROCK THE HOSPITAL	137
WHAT A DAY THIS HAS BEEN	139
WORKING DAYS	142
Other Books by Author	145

PART I
BOOKS

GOTHAM NIGHTS

This poem was inspired by DC comics'
BATMAN

Gotham Nights will drive you crazy.
Gotham Nights, they'll drive you mad.
Strange things happen upon these streets,
and every story is very sad.

Gotham's normal people
live their lives during the day.
But the slime of Gotham
live their lives another way.

Preying on the weak
and stabbings in the back,
Gotham's nighttime dwellers
wait in shadows to attack.
Young girls will walk the night,

while old men drink it down,
the boys fight like cocks,
and old women, they make no sounds.

I knew a little girl
whose parents, they both died.
They left her alone in the world,
but for them, she did not cry.

She spent her nights upon the streets
and she learned her trade like that.
Now that she's all grown up,
she owns the night as the woman cat.

Gotham Nights will drive you mad,
upon your life, they'll take their toll.
Gotham Nights will drive you crazy,
and they'll take away your soul.

When Jack was just a young man,
he danced with the Devil, in the pale moon light.
But now Batman's gotten to him,
and his face is a green and jovial sight.

As the Joker, he'll terrorize you,
with his deadly pranks.
While he laughs the night away,
pumping laughing gas into Gotham banks.

Gotham Nights will drive you insane,
unless you have a heart of stone.
They not for normal men,
made of flesh and bone.
You must be extraordinary
to walk the Gotham streets at night.
Just like the caped crusader
who, against crime, leads the fight.

Sgt. Bullock doesn't like him,
and neither to do the crooks.
But it's Commissioner Gordon
who puts away what Batman hooks.

Batman, Gotham's faithful dark knight,
is vigilant twenty-four hours a day.
And with him upon Gotham's streets felons never get away.

HEARTS OF SNOW

A cold winter's night a mother was drunk
   and told her two children they were nothing, but punks.
   Cries were uttered as slaps were given,
   The Queen took them away
   to the North they were driven.

   Hearts of snow, they bloom, and they fall
   they soar to the sky and become nothing at all.
   All hail the Queen as she takes them away.
   Hearts of snow, and so full of pain.

   It was a gloomy winter's morning when I went to see Kay,
   His father had beaten him and told him no more to play.

We both wished hard that night to fly far away.

All hail the Queen, She saved us both that day.
Hearts of snow, they bloom, and they fall
they soar to the sky and become nothing at all.
All hail the Queen as she takes them away.
Hearts of snow, and so full of pain.

SABINA HALL

This poem was inspired by Sherlock Holmes
and
The Case of Sabina Hall written by L.B. Greenwood.

An old friend writes to Holmes a doctor to find
   He tells him to hurry for time, to his uncle
   is most unkind.

As Holmes reads the letter, his curiosity peaks
   who are all these people,
   of which his friend speaks.

Miss Garth, Miss Meredith, The harpers
Old Silas, Old Ned, and young Sally Kipp;
He wonders why they are all there
as he and Watson prepare for the trip.

    Miss Garth is as an undone pie.
    Miss Meredith is as dice, missing one die.
    Old Silas is just like a star is at a new day.
    Old Ned is like a shadow that just won't go away.

    Belle and Joel Harper are treated as slaves,
    and Sally is here, who knows why she stays.
    Just as Holmes and Watson arrive
    Poor old Andrew Silas – he dies.
    by poison Holmes doth decree,
    but miss Garth is indifferent, she is as iced tea.

    "Hurry up and read the will
    I will stay here no more
    with my inheritance, I will get
    away from this godforsaken shore"

    Holmes is puzzled,
    Watson is stunned.

    "Who would want to poison him?"

"Come Watson, The game has begun."

A missing horse, Seaweed in the shed,
Footprints in the snow, and now miss Garth is found dead.
"Egad, another murder?!" cried Watson.
"Watson, you twit. I am a great fool.
There are now not one murder, but two.
and for the life of me I still don't know who.
or Why."

"Well, Holmes the deed is done
and we know how. The only question I have is
What do we do now?"
"Young Sally, she knows something. She is the key,
if only she would talk to you
or confide to in me."

Then —
Belle flees into the night.
Joel brings her back, there is a big fight.

A half empty bottle, A whorehouse, a raid.
A man, A woman, and an unborn new babe.
"This tale grows twisted the more I doth try.
I need more clues, or this case will stump even I."
Through the vicar, Holmes finds out
How and why Miss Garth came to stay.
And through old newspapers he now knows
Joel and Belle's reason too — But to his dismay,
He knows young sally kipp is in grave danger,
and the one who will kill her – will not be a stranger.
"Meet me at the old mine"
Sally doth plead.
"and there I will tell you all that you need."

Holmes runs to meet her – he hopes to find her alive.
But Watson identifies the marks on her body
"She was not struck once, but five times."

He is too late, and she is dead.
He would have been too, if the cave in had fell on his head.

Into the night, a figure runs
Holmes and Watson do now doth pursue
The figure is caught, but for miss Meredith it's not very good news.

The murder is Holmes' old friend, and her husband to be.
Who will be tried and convicted for the murder of not one person, but three.

WHAT KIND OF A MAN?

This poem was inspired by Ian Fleming's James Bond.

What kind of a man do you want to know?
What kind of a man is more valued than gold?
What kind of a man has an ego like snow?
Only a man like James Bond could ever fit the mold.

One look into his eyes
Tells you he's danger.
One touch of his hand
and you won't care.
One brush of his lips
and for you, it's all over.
One moment in time
is more than you can bare.

What kind of a man can jump a cycle over a plane?

What kind of a man will place a tank in front of a train?

What kind of a man wins dog fights with boats?

Only a man like James Bond with a glance, a heart he can smote.

One look into his eyes
Tells you he's danger.
One touch of his hand
and you won't care.
One brush of his lips
and for you, it's all over.
One moment in time
is more than you can bare.

What kind of a man drives a car like a demon?

What kind of a man can you trust and believe in?

What kind of a man thinks fast on his feet?

Only a man like James Bond will evil – never defeat!

PART II
BI-LINGUAL

DIVERTIDO

Divertido, I love to play.
   Divertido, on every day.
   Divertido, I love to sing.
   I'd rather play, than anything.

   Divertido, I love to danza.
   Play the guitarra, and do the somba.
   Divertido, I am this way. And
   Divertido, I will stay.

   Simpre juego little children, never stop having fun.
   Because the day that you do, your fun is forever done.
   For an adult you will be, all rigid and stiff,
   and easily tick off at every little tiff.

   So simpre divertido, fiesta, party, and play.
   Always have mucho fun, every hour of every day.

NADA ES ME CULPA

by Tracy Taylor & Wendy Cevallos

Nada es me culpa, Nothing is my fault.
Yet everything I say, is taken with grains of salt.
I know it's not wrong, if I do it this way.
Todo es Su culpa, I know is what she'll say.
First my boss tells me, "Do this." but how she doesn't say,
Yet by the time I'm finish, she'll tell me another way.

Aiy,Aiy,Aiy,Aiy
No es me culpa.
This is not my fault,
but she'll tell me I am wrong.

My husband he loves me, but yet when we fight,
some how it ends up, that he's always right.
We'll argue and yell for more than half the night.
And when it's all over, we'll stay from each other's sight.

Aiy,Aiy,Aiy,Aiy
Nada es me culpa.
Tengo dolor de cabeza,
My head is hurting,
as I sing my canción.

My best friend and I, we always get along.
But when we disagree, I am always wrong.
I will say yes, and she will say no.
I'll want to stay, and she'll want to go.

Aiy,Aiy,Aiy,Aiy
No es my culpa.
This is not my fault,
but she'll tell me I'm wrong.

Aiy,Aiy,Aiy,Aiy Nada es me culpa.
Tengo dolor de cabeza,
My head is hurting, as I sing my canción.

QUE ES SU PROBLEMA?

Que es su problema?
   Why blame this on me?
   I was here first, you know.
   So you will have to leave.

   Que es su problema?
   Just what is it with you?
   The speed limit is fifty-five,
   and I see lights – red and blue.

   Que es su problema?
   You know it was not me.
   No es me culpa
   I drive as safe as I can be.

   Que es me problema?
   My teacher says to me.
   I'd better stay awake in class,

or I'll get another "D".

Que es me problema?
Sometimes I do not know.
My friends all think I'm crazy,
y me madre says "tu estas loco."

Sometimes I am half awake,
when I dream that I am sleep.
And when I dream about her
I know I'm in trouble deep.

For she is there to warn me,
about what lies beyond the door.
And just when I think I've got it,
I wake up on the floor.

Que es su problema?
What is it that bothers you?
What kind of things make you mad
and burn a reddish hue.

Sometimes a problem is very big, or it may be really small.

El mundo esta lleno de problemas, and full of worries for us all.

PART III
CHURCH

EASTER SUNDAY

One day about 2,030 years ago,
   God became a man to save lost souls.
   The day he was born, he knew that he would die.
   For the sins of us all, both you and I.

   Thirty-three years later, that fateful day came.
   When upon the cross Jesus Christ was slain.
   Soldiers spat upon him, and gave him a crown of thorns.
   As his disciples watched in sadness, what else could they do, but morn.

   The devil himself was in attendance that day.
   "Now," he thought, "I will be Lord." As our savior passed away.

The day Jesus died, the sun hid its face,
and the veil rent in twain at the temple place.

But here the story does not end.
For the battle between darkness and light was about to begin.
When Jesus died, he passed through death's door.
Paying the price for our sins forever more.

But that is not all that he did in his plan, our lives to save.
He went straight to hell and took back his keys to death and the grave.
The devil and his demons partied hard and drank even more.
But suddenly there came a knock upon the door.

"Whoever it is, Let them in." ordered the devil with a great big grin.
Then in through the door walked our Lord.
The devil stood still and his jaw hit the floor.

"I've come for my keys to death and the grave.
The debt has been paid and mankind is saved."
"No, I saw you die, shrouded in sin."
"I lay down my life and I take it back up again."

"Uhh, that maybe, but these keys are mine.
And your shed blood is not the only fine.
The only way to get these keys,
is over my cold and dead body."

And so for three days and three nights,
in the depths of hell was a terrible fight.
But on that day of Easter morning,
there stood two women, all forlorning.

The tomb was open and the Lord's body was missin'.
Then an angel appeared and said to me please listen.
"Here is where he lay, but not anymore.

With his resurrection, he has fulfilled the law.
Now go tell the disciples, one and all
to go to Galilee and wait for his call."

And since that day, we have been saved
from the sting of death, hell, and the grave.
With repentance, all our sins are forgiven.
With baptism, a brand-new life, unto us, is given.

So, when you feel lost, depressed, and misunderstood.
Just look at the cross and remember the good.
Our heavenly father, who is but one.
Who gave of himself and his only son.

THE GOOD SHEPHERD

Once upon a time, there was a Shepherd with sheep.

He kept a watchful guard, while they did eat and sleep.

Wolves and bears and lions he killed.

His one duty was the sheep's good will.

But then one day, a lamb got lost.

He was left behind as he lay in the moss.

The good Shepherd knew that being lost is no fun.

So he left the ninety-nine to go search for the one.

Searching everyday and searching every night,

He sought the lost lamb, with all of his might.

Climbing mountains high, and searching valleys low,
   to find this one lost lamb, was his only goal.

Several days later, upon this little lamb, he finally came,
   but it was cold and hungry and it was terribly lame.
   With sweet gentility and great care,
   he lifted the little lamb high into the air.
   Upon his shoulders, this lamb he did carry,
   while singing praises to God and his heart did make merry.

So all good Shepherds are gentle and kind.
   They heal the wounds and lamb's enemies bind.
   All good Shepherds are bold and brave,
   they protect the flock and seek lost ones to save.

Such a Shepherd, my Great Lord, has given to me
   and his name is Pastor Jonathan Kelly.

Like a good Shepherd, he watches out for me.
Like a good soldier, he fights keeping my soul free.

He prays day and night for the souls of his flock,
while the lessons of the bible, for them he unlocks.
He lifts us up, whenever we stumble
and he instructs us, to keep us from fumbles.
He is strong in character and of a willing spirit.
He feeds us God's word and urges us to hear it.

God's word says, "If you love me, feed my sheep."
And this our Pastor does, even though we may bleat.
"I don't want to, I can't, and It's not fair."
But as sheep, you can't see what's out there.
But as our Pastor and Shepherd, I believe

Rev. Jonathan Kelly does.

And I assure you he does it with all honesty and love.

For this job of Shepherd, is not an easy position.

He could have easily gone to a game or gone out fishing.

But he loves us and God, with all of his heart.

So from this position, he will not depart.

Though the lack of tithes and offerings may his wallet dent.

He won't stop till God says, "Well done, my good and faithful servant."

So, on this day of Pastor Appreciation

I bring you thanks from God's peculiar nation.

I thank you, sir, for not deserting your post

and for delivering my soul unto our Great Host.

THE MAN FROM GALILEE

He was born one evening, on a cold winter's night.
 Only wise men, sheep, and shepherds, ever saw the sight.
 They followed a star, that in the sky did shine,
 showing here is the place and now is the time.
 They brought him presents and bowed to their king,
 while the angels rejoiced and in heaven did sing.

 By the time he was twelve, he was teaching in church.
 But his parents thought him lost and they began to search.

In the synagogue, his words, with attention they pay

His parents scolded him, but to them he did say.

Marvel not at what I do, and this is no lie

about my father's business, there go I.

To the men of the temple, he said Good day,

As his mother and father just led him away.

At age thirty-three, he was ready to go.

To tell people about The God, they should know.

He chose twelve men to be his friends

and to him they swore, We'll stay till the end.

They roamed the land and they did good deeds,

they spread God's word and they sowed the seeds.

James, John, and Peter watched him walk though the land,

giving the sick and the needy a hand.

He fed five thousand on two fishes and bread,

he walked on the water and he raised the dead.
He turned water into wine, and he calmed the raging sea,
and wherever he went, people came to see
this wonderful man, the man from Galilee.

One day, a town threw a gal at his feet and
thousands of charges they began to bleat.
Jesus looked kindly upon this woman of sin
then asked them why they had brought her to him.
Her charge is this, with men she doth lie
she is not married, so now she must die.

He said not a word, but wrote in the sludge.
They just stood – waiting for him to judge.
Without looking up, he said – First you must atone.
Let those without guilt, cast the first stone.
They looked around, but they couldn't lie
and one by one, they all said Goodbye.

When Jesus looked up, not a one he saw

all the girl's accusers had left and gone.
Jesus looked at her, right straight to the core,
he said, be thou gone and sin no more.

Who is this man? This man from Galilee,
who roams the world from Jordan and to the dead sea.
Teaching his disciples how to feed his sheep,
and drying the eyes of all the ones who weep.
Healing the sick, the blind, and the lame,
He is God, the almighty, the one and the same.

MY HEAVENLY FATHER

Soft and graceful, steady and slow,
   Never too fast and never on the go.
   Never in a hurry and never at a loss,
   loves me so much, that he died on a cross.

   With arms full of love,
   and a face full of light,
   ever quietly listening
   I'm safe from the night.

   Quiet, cheerful, loving and nice,
   Peaceful and gentle, caring and wise.
   Warm and kind, with patient eyes.
   Never forceful and never lies.
   I have nothing to worry
   and nothing to fear
   when my Heavenly Father
   is close and near.

REJOICE

Rejoice in celebration as the sun brings on the day.

Rejoice in celebration as the moon and night slip away.

Rejoice in celebration as another day is born.

Rejoice in celebration at the coming of the morn.

The skies are blue and clear just like the glorious sea.

With the perfect love of God, who made them just for me.

The trees rejoice as well, as the wind blows through leaves.

Uplifting the name of the one God, in whom all the world believes.

Rejoice in celebration as the birds of heaven sing.

Rejoice in celebration as the grass of earth doth swing.
Rejoice in celebration as life begins anew.
Rejoice in celebration as in the love of God, you grew.

Rejoice is celebration as you live another day.
Rejoice is celebration as all fear is chased away.
Rejoice in celebration for the Lord, he is strong.
Rejoice in celebration as He protects you from all wrong.

Rejoice in celebration as the moon brings on the night.
Rejoice in celebration as sleeping children, do not fight.
Rejoice in celebration as another night is abreast.
Rejoice in celebration as you lay your head in rest.

The night is inky and black
and the stars shine down from above.
God put them there for you and me
so that we might fall in love.

O' the awesome wonder
of the sky at night.
It goes on into forever,
far reaching the blessed light.

Rejoice in celebration as the rain gently falls.
Rejoice in celebration at the owl's nightly calls.
Rejoice in celebration as all the day ones go to sleep.
Rejoice in celebration as flowers drink in the rain that seeps.

Rejoice is celebration as you rest another night.
Rejoice is celebration forget the day and its plights.

Rejoice in celebration as the Lord, your life did bleed.

Rejoice in celebration as your life, he will never leave.

SHOW ME THE WAY

Show me the way, as I walk through this land.
   Show me the way, O, Lord Jesus, hold my hand.
   Show me the way; Guide me by your light.
   Show me the way, Guide me through the night.

   Show me the way, for I am very young.
   Show me the way, for to the Lions, I am flung.
   Show me the way, Guide me and Lead me.
   Show me the way, because Lord, I need thee.

   Show me the way, when I grow old.
   Show me the way, to your land of gold.
   Show me the way, to the land of your care.
   Show me the way, So that I may rest there.

THANK YOU, JESUS THANK YOU

Chorus:
Thank you, Jesus, Thank you.
Thank you, Jesus, Thank you.
Thank you, Jesus, Thank you.
Hallelujah and praise the Lord.

Verse 1:
When things do go wrong,
don't sit and have a fit.
Just lift your hands and praise the Lord,
and let God take care of it.

Verse 2:
The Devil tries his best
to sow discord and unrest.
But no matter what he throws at me,

God helps me pass the test.

THE TRIAL

"Poppycock" he said, and his eyes became grim.
 Dark as storm clouds they were, and as red as the color of sin.

 He did not believe me even though I told the truth.
 And I began to sweat as I sat in the judgment booth.
 I swallowed hard as the jury I did scan.
 There was not smile among them, not a woman or a man.

 Question upon question did they asked of me,
 my hands were soaking wet, and my heart began to bleed.

 My soul became very heavy, and my throat began to dry.

A liar to my face he called me, and I began to cry.

"It's the truth," I cried. "as I've been sworn to give.
Upon a floating city, in the sky I did live."

I told them of much beauty and about abundant joy.
I told them about the happiness of each girl and boy.
And when the end of all my story, I had told.
He looked at me and smiled with three teeth, all of gold.

"So young man, if all this be true.
How come you live down here beneath your sky of blue?"

"Because dear sir, I am ... just like you.
I did not cover my sins, with His blood of scarlet hue."

His smile died and so did his glee.

He just sat there, staring straight at me.

I didn't know what to say Or what, to me, he would do.
So I just sat there also, staring at him too.

"Step down, young man", he said. "And take your … "honored" place.
With all the other unforgiven, upon the field of disgrace."

So now here I reside, in a place, so Goddamned.
Staring at a great gulf, and dreaming of another land.

PART IV
DEATH

THE COLOR OF DOOM

Black is the night, Gold is the moon
    Red is the ground; Blue is the groom.
    White are the teeth, Brown is his hair
    Odd is the sound that hangs in the air.

    The wind whispers and death stalks
    While willows cry and owls do talk.
    Who died? Who is lost?
    Who lies here among the moss.

    I say nothing, not a word.
    Who told me all this?
    A little bird.

I MISS MY LIFE, MY LOVE

I miss my life, my love
    I miss my mom and I miss my dad.
    I miss my life, my love
    I miss you and the fun we had.

    I miss my life, my love
    I miss baseball games, and my hat.
    I miss my life, my love
    and comic books, like "Gunsmith Cats".

    I miss rainy days and starry nights,
    MTV and John Wayne fights.
    I miss skateboards and roller blades,
    my faded blue jeans and my pilots' shades.

    But most of all I miss you
    and all the fun things we used to do.

Like riding dirt bikes and mountain climbing,
white water rafting and deep sea diving.

I miss late night movies and our long talks.
I miss your laugh and the dead mummy walk.
I miss your touch and your loving kiss.
Remembering this brings tears and bliss.

I miss my life, my love
but in my heart, I miss you sore.
And I would give my life, my love
to be with you forevermore.

SAM'S DAY

The rain fell. The wind blew.
   My heart was cold, and my arms missed you.
   The rain fell, as I cried.
   I was alone now; my love had died.

   The rain fell and it hid my tears.
   As I thought about, our twenty years

   As the rain fell, the reverend said a prayer.
   I said one too, in this cold morning air.

   I was glad that it was raining
   As the heavens cried for Sam.
   He was everything to me, and made me what I am.

PART V
LOVE

FOR THE LOVE OF ROSES

Roses are red, what more can I say.
True love, they present, in a beautiful way.
Their blooms are red, and their stems green,
but thorny they are, you know what I mean.
Good and bad, both, combine,
they bloom for a season,
they grow together in time.
Like people, in nature,
they grow and they die.
They are given in love,
and they make you cry.

MY NEW LOVE

His eyes were blue and misty, like the dawning of a day.

His kisses were like candy, and they took my breath away.

His hands as they caressed me, made me long for more.

My heart began to race away, as we lay upon the floor.

A glorious day became a magnificent night.

As we talked, we played, and we'd pillow-fight.

I didn't want the day to end, but it did, as all things do.

And as you said, Goodbye, that day you swore your love was true.

My heart was still soaring as you slowly walked away.

By love, I had been bound and my apprehensions kept at bay.

I thought nothing of tomorrow, only wishing more of today.

ON MY WEDDING DAY

What Have I done?! What did I just do?!
What on this Earth ever possessed me to say I do.

What was I thinking?! I must have been out of my mind
What a great power, this thing love, to keep me so giddy and blind.

I swore never to fall in love and I swore never to marry.
Both these vows I have broken and yet my heart is more merry.
It's something about him that makes my heart soar.
For each time I see him, I just want to be with him more.

His eyes are dark brown and speak volumes to me.

His hugs are like fuel blasting my restless soul free.

My Pride demanded of me. Just say no!

But my lonely heart cried out. Please don't let him go.

For so long we were alone, but I liked it that way

I did what I wanted – when I wanted and no one, but me, had a say.

But Today – that all changed, my maiden days are done.

With those two words – I do, we are now a different One.

My heart is in the air and yet my knees are on the floor.

I want to stand beside him, but my eyes are on the door.

I want to run away; I just want to flee.

I don't want wifely duties, or any responsibilities.

But just when I think I have the courage to leave.
He smiles at me brightly, and whispers, In you I believe.
Who am I kidding? I've been running for so long.
And each step away I took, I knew that I was wrong.

So now I say I do, with all my heart and soul.
And I swear to you to fulfill, with love, my new role.

For only in your arms am I truly free.
And here beside you, my love is where I long to be.

QUIET PONDERINGS

Did I find you? or did God lead me here.
   Do you know who I am?
   Do you even really care?

   I smile when I think of you.
   I laugh at thoughts so impure.
   I wish I could be with you.
   I sigh, as lonely nights, I endure.

   For in your eyes, I have seen passion and desire,
   a lust for adventure rages, from within, like fire.
   This longing for travel, we could share,
   if only you understood, that for you, I do care.
   But you, I must regret
   don't feel the same way yet.

So for now, I must wait;
but mind you lad, not too late.
For you to look and see me
and the lover, that I could be.

SQUISHY FEELINGS

It's strange how I feel when I think about you.

It's like sitting in water and your feet without shoes.

It's like wet paste as it sticks to your hands.

Or like the soft and wet stuff in empty peach cans.

It's strange how my thoughts carry me away.

Straying far from me, like young children at play.

Thoughts, slowly drifting like music in the air.

Softly sighing and dreaming of a world without care.

It's strange how it sounds all quiet and serine.

Babbling water, tweeting birds, skies of blue and trees of green.

Like sweet water taffy and Mary Janes, sticky, sweet, chewy and good,

Like after it rains and then you put on your hood.

It's strange how I feel when I think about you.

My stomach wiggles, my fingers get wet and my mouth feels like glue.

It's a strange anticipation like worry and dread.

Like orange juice and lollipops, or jelly on bread.

TEASING THOUGHTS

He walked into my room, late that night.
   His underwear fit good and tight.
   O' that I would have the might
   to fulfill my longing wish tonight.

   But did I have the strength to dare.
   About what mother said, I did not care.
   We rode, that night upon a mare,
   into a place called Nowhere.

   The next morning, I returned
   from a place I could not discern.
   It was asked of me where I had been.
   Should I tell them...The Garden of Eden.

WHAT MIGHT HAVE BEEN

I looked into the sky that night
   Impressed by the stars' and their twinkling lights.
   Saddened though by the thought of you
   and the one act of love, that we can never do.

   Like comets, we played fast and hard.
   Laughing at life and it's cruel shards.
   Daring to challenge space and time,
   as we pledged, each other, our hearts and minds.

   In mind, thought, and deed
   we acted as we were one.
   Our passion and love
   Disgracefully, shaming the sun.
   Running throughout the universe

with nothing, but our love of verse.

With Shakespeare as our porter,
and Dickenson our muse,
As Milton is our conscience,
all our virtues we would lose.

Or so we had hoped,
but in the end,
Our virtue won us over
and we are naught, but friends.

WILD ONE

Love is a real high gamble,
    With many hits and decks.
    It can leave your heart in ecstasy
    Or a cold and lonely wreck.
    Win with hearts and diamonds,
    Lose with clubs and spades,
    Draw with ladies wild, or
    Pass on love's sharp blade.

PART VI
PERSONS

CYNTHA J.

Cynthia J. paved the way for women everywhere.
   For what she did she did not care,
   as long as we were treated fair.

   She loved her man and her job.
   She loved her child, a boy named Rob.
   She paved their way with food and love
   and prayed each day to the Father above.

   Cynthia J. tall and strong, was a woman kind.
   But if you dare to make her mad,
   She'll always lose her mind.

IAN

The day of Ian, was the day you were born.

When the angels of heaven blew their tin horns.

They shouted "Look out below, here he comes...

If they had any brains, they'd get up and run."

The day we met, we became friends
and now share a love, I hope never ends.
Cause to be with you – is such a blast.
Dreaming of our future, while laughing at our past.

Paris was fun, but my place was funner.
Us together is like watching dumb and dumber.
We have fun, like nobody else has
because you are so cool, just like hot jazz.

To say our love is like a rose is sweet,
or like a lotto ticket that the odds beat.
To be with you always, is what I want.
And if I were dead, your place I'd haunt.

Sharing life, love, and an occasional bath,
it's your bright smile that makes me laugh.
To know that you care, is such a good feeling.
It sends my head and my heart reeling.

And so, to honor the day of your birth,
I raise my glass and say with great mirth.
That I'm glad and overjoyed that your here,
Now pull out a twenty and pay for the beer.

SAM'S LULLABY

Go to sleep, my little lamb.
   Sail to dreamland, my little Sam.
   Lay down your head and close your eyes.
   Let go all your questions, ask no more whys.
   Why?
   Shush.
   Go to sleep, my little dear.
   Do not cry, I am right here.
   Dream, Sweet Dreams, full of delights.
   Sleep well, sleep fast, sleep long, sleep tight.

STEPHEN M

Why do I love him? I don't know.

Why does my admiration cause my love to grow?

When I look at him, what do I see?

A brilliant young man, and a musician to be.

What spell, over me, has he cast?

Why, for him only, does my heart beat fast?

Why does his being haunt me in my dreams?

What, myself I ask, does it all mean?

Why do I care so much for one man?

Will he ever be there?

I just don't understand.

Why can't he see, what it is, that he does to me?

And why on earth can't I be, in control of my perplexity.

THOMAS L.

This is the tale of Thomas Li,
   He worked for ATS.
   Tomorrow will be his last day here,
   and I wish him all the best.

   Thomas Li did his job well,
   he was kind, dedicated, and true.
   He was a real ingenious engineer,
   and stuck to his computer like glue.

   He did his job without complaining,
   he worked long hours into the night.
   He created programs without bugs,
   and freed FAA from their plights.

   To Thomas Li, a real good friend.
   Good luck, best wishes, and farewell.
   It's been a ball, it's been great fun,
   now go on out and give them hell.

PART VII
REFLECTIONS

BENEATH THE WATERFALL

In the woods ancient and deep,
   Where all creation comes to weep.
   Into the river, it becomes a waterfall
   full of the sorrows of us all.

   But at noon, when the sun is high,
   all prayers are answered, and peace is a sigh.
   Beneath this waterfall, I come to play
   All fear, all hate, all pain it drives away.

   When I see the water crystal clear and full of sun,
   all creation, I know, is made by one.
   When I hear the roar of the water as it falls,
   His voice I hear, to me he calls.

When I smell the clean crisp air the water makes
(and understanding what it takes)
I can forgive other men's mistakes.

When I taste the water dew,
My thirst is quenched, my life renewed.
When I feel the water over me it flows,
Away it washes all the blows.

Thus, refreshed and forgiven,
again the world I can live in.

LIKE CHILDREN

Why can't we be like Children?
   who believe in everything.
   For whom nothing is impossible,
   we'd play, have fun and sing.
   Where anger only lasts a minute,
   and then, forever, it is no more.

   Why can't we be like children?
   as they play upon the floor.

   Why can't be like children?
   Where violence we can resist.
   And everybody is a friend,
   Where race and color do not exist.
   We would have no such worries,
   to cause us great distress,
   So why can't we be like children,
   with few fears, to hinder our progress.

   Why can't we be like children?

who seek to know how and why,
the sky is blue, the days are long,
and how can scrapers touch the sky.
To whom Harmony is a mother,
and Rhythm is a dad.
Where music is our language,
and wonder is our land.

NIGHT DREAMING

One starry night, I lay,
   Looking up at the sky.
   Wishing I could be
   A comet or a firefly.
   Zooming cross the cosmos,
   Playing on planets old,
   Burning out at day break,
   Dying in the cold.
   Living fast and hard
   Living on forever
   In the evening sky
   Riding on Endeavor.

TAUGHT TO CARE

I saw a star fall, but I just let it lay.
 I heard it call for help. But I just walked away.

 It begged and it pleaded, put me back in the air.
 It's the one who fell down so why should I care.

 But something inside me wouldn't let me go.
 I had to help the star I couldn't say no.

 So, I reached down and picked it up with such care.
 And then I gave a great toss throwing it back into the air.

Away into the night it flew as happy as can be.

I was happy now also because I had been set free.

WHAT WILL THIS DAY BRING?

I see clouds of blue and a road of black
   tall brown trees and a white Cadillac
   I hear birds and they love to sing
   Tell me now what will this day bring?

   I got two feet that hit the ground and
   I like the view as I look around
   The day is good and so is the sun
   upon the streets, I'm not the only one.
   There are men, and animals, and cars and things
   Tell me now what will this day bring?

   I'm feeling good and I'm feeling fine.
   Got out of bed at a quarter to nine.
   I found ten dollars just lying in the street

I've gotta wicked rhythm and a really cool beat.
Such a great morning with a lot of zing,
Got to wonder what will this day bring?

Lucky in Lotto or unlucky in love,
either way I say thank you to the Lord above.
His hands guide me gentle and they guide me true.

He guides me sure as the sky is blue.
He loves me so much, I just gotta sing.
Tell me Lord, what will this day bring.
The day could be good, or the day could be bad.
The day could be the best that I've ever had
The sun could be shinning, or It could be rain.
I could be healthy, or I could be in pain.
Or my love could bring me a diamond ring
so tell me quickly now, what will this day bring?

I stand and wonder what will this day bring?

But it really doesn't matter, cause I love to sing.

Hallelujah, thank you Lord for everything

You made me loving, cheerful, and full of zing

But what about my love with his diamond ring?

Please, I ask you, tell me what will this day bring?

PART VIII
SILLY THINGS

BOTTLES AND CANS

Space ships and Launching Pads.
   But all I see are bottles and cans.
   Great big castles in the sand.
   But all I see are bottles and cans.

   Soldiers marching across the dunes.
   But all I see are bottles and cans.
   Hallow drums for making tunes.
   But all I see are bottles and cans.

   Oh, come now, use your imagination.
   Surely you must have a little some.
   Check your pockets, behind your gum.
   Look the train's pulling in the station.

   Glimmering fingers of a giant
   But all I see are bottles and cans.
   Musical instruments for a small band.

But all I see are bottles and cans.

One more time, if you please.
Close your eyes and think on these,
Shiny trees without their leaves
Or maybe even ships on high seas.

Now I get it, they are cylinder houses.
Or tiny jails for angry spouses.
They are compasses that can spin,
Or maybe they are bowling pins.

That's it dear, that's the game.
I like this one. What's its name?
Anything that you want it to be,
But bottles and cans is good for me.

CHRISTMAS COUNTING

12 points of light, in the evening sky.
  11 friends have I, drinking Kentucky rye.
  10 says the clock, in the dining room.
  9 is the channel, Scrooge sees his tomb.
  8 candles burning, dancing light at play.
  7 angels sleeping, each one a day.
  6 pizza boxes, empty and cold.
  5 lambs near the manger, beneath a star of gold.
  4 carolers outside, singing in the snow.
  3 stockings hung, waiting for – you know.
  2 mistletoes, hanging on the wall.
  1 Christmas tree, lighted, standing tall.

HAPPY ROCK-N-ROLLERS

A happy rock-n-roller is what I am.
   I love to play guitar and I love to Jam.
   A man once told us – the future's in your hands,
   that's why we got together and formed this band.

   Happy rock-n-rollers is what we are,
   playing all gigs, whether near or far.
   A happy rock-n-roller is the way to be,
   playing our music on MTV.

   Here Kitty, Kitty, is what they say.
   Come and play some tunes now, right away.
   Cause the party's gettin' hot and It's no lie.

We're happy rock-n-rollers till the day we die.

Happy rock-n-rollers is what we are,
playing all gigs, whether near or far.
A happy rock-n-roller is the way to be,
playing our music on MTV.

Gotta stay clean, Cops are keeping a tab.
They got square jaws, and they don't pull jabs.
Jails no place to be, cause you can't rock there.
And if I can't rock, I'll pull out my hair.

Happy rock-n-rollers is what we are,
playing all gigs, whether near or far.
A happy rock-n-roller is the way to be,
playing our music on MTV.

KENTUCKY WINE

I'm going to get some fine Kentucky wine
   I'm going to get some fine Kentucky wine
   I'm going to get some fine Kentucky wine,
   and have a party tonight.

   George brought chicken and turkey.
   Tom brought cheese and bread.
   Lucy brought apples and oranges.
   Betty brought Charles and he brought Fred.

   We're going to eat and drink and dance, all night.
   Bet a lot money on the big cock fight
   and tease married men about their plight,
   Until the early morning light.

   George went home at 6:00 am.
   Tom went home at 8:00.

Betty went home at noon time,
But Lucy didn't go till it was late.

12 kegs of fine Kentucky wine, we drank till we were through.

Charles and Fred slept on the floor, and didn't wake up till it was June.

MICE SLAYERS

We roam the night in search of our prey.
    We hide our faces from the light of day.
    We wear the darkness like a cloak,
    distress the cops and get their goats.

    Mice Slayers
    We are nobody's fools.
    Mice Slayers
    We don't live life, by their rules.
    Mice Slayers
    We are the masters of the night.
    Mice Slayers
    We rock and roll until the morning light.
    We rock and roll until the morning light.
    Don't live our lives by ticks and tocks.
    In fact, we smashed up all our clocks.
    As a pride, we roam the night as one,
    until the morning...brings up the sun.

    Mice Slayers

We are nobody's fools.
Mice Slayers
We don't live life by their rules.
Mice Slayers
We are the masters of the night.
Mice Slayers
We rock and roll until the morning light.
We rock and roll until the morning light.

We are children of the night, shunned by those who live in
light.
Together, as one, we will strive. Together .... we will survive.

Mice Slayers
is the name of our band.
Mice Slayers
our future lies in our hands.
Mice Slayers
We Rock and Roll our music hard.
Mice Slayers
We are life's wildest cards.
We are life's wildest cards.

MY RAT

My dad caught a Rat and gave it to me.
    Our cat chased the Rat, and I named it Lee.

    Lee the Rat is my pet. He smells bad when he gets wet.
    Lee the Rat He likes cheese. And our cat He likes to tease.
    Lee the Rat He is smart.
    All the mousetraps he can dart.

    Lee the Rat He is my friend.
    And I will keep him till the end.
    Or at least until our cat, catches hold of him.

THE OCEAN

The Ocean swallowed my mother.
   The Ocean swallowed my dad.
   The Ocean swallowed their ship up.
   Now, I think the Ocean is bad.

   The Sea beat against the ship.
   The Sea beat against the men.
   The Sea beat against the decks.
   O, what a time it has been.

   The waters are rising.
   The ship is sinking.
   The men are drowning.
   A lighthouse is blinking.

   The ship is now gone.
   The men are now dead.
   Now aren't you glad
   This poem you've read.

TAKE YOUR DISHES WITH YOU

Take your dishes with you into the kitchen – Please.

    Take your dishes with you cause we don't need ticks and flees.

    Take your dishes with you take them out of your room.

    And when you make your way back, best you bring a broom.

    Take your dishes with you that's a bad habit, that you got.

    Take your dishes with you Do it now! Before the dishes rot.

    Into the kitchen with your dishes!
    Now your making me mad.
    Take those dishes into the kitchen

or by God, you'll wish you had.

Take those dishes into the kitchen I'll not tell you twice.
Your maid does not live here, and we don't leave food for mice.
Take those dishes into the kitchen, Now!
And don't do this no more.
I catch you eating in your room again and I'll put you out the door.

THAT DAY

I can see you, and all that you do.

You're in trouble buddy, like a rabbit in a stew.

I know what you are thinking, but what can you bring?

That would atone for what you did, when you left up the toilet lid.

I thought that I loved you, but this, I cannot forgive.

What you did was inconsiderate, and I don't think that you should live.

However, small this matter is, compared to yesterday,

when with an airline stewardess you tried to run-away.

How long will you go on like this?

My love you have forsaken.

And though I loved you once, my dear.

I will cook your butt like bacon!

THE WED OF ROCK AND CLASSICAL

When I was a little girl, I did play classical.
But I didn't like the pace, it was boring, it was slow.
Then I found a brand new beat.
Now with the drums, I move my feet.
It's got rhythm. It's got soul. And –
it's called Rock-N-Roll.
But my mother said no way.
Rock-n-Roll, It cannot stay
From classical don't stray.
You must practice every day.
So, I practiced every day from Chopin to Bizet,
From Vivaldi's Rite of Spring to the Halls of Mountain King.
But all the while, in my soul

came a cry for Rock-n-Roll.

Now I played Mozart and some Bach
to the beat of modern Rock.
I heard them roll in their graves
as their music faster played.

I play now classical to the beat of Rock-n-Roll.
As I play, I need a hand, so I formed a brand new band.
With the masters as foundation, we became Time Violation.
So now mother says O.K.
As classical I play
in 2 – 4 time my way
to the crowds as they yell Yeah!

This song now I do call
the Wed of Rock and Classical.
The combo of Beethoven and
Bon Jovi played hand in hand.

PART IX
TELEVISION SHOWS

BLACK VANS AND HELICOPTERS

This poem was inspired by episodes of The X-Files.

    Black Vans and Helicopters are messengers of the night.
    Black Vans and Helicopters care nothing for wrong or right.
    Black Vans and Helicopters come to save us from unknown fears.
    Black Vans and Helicopters just leave us with our tears.

    G-men got the Martians and G-men got the freaks
    G-men got the Pres. watching reruns of Twin Peaks.

G-man even got my neighbor looking out for me.

But the G-man cannot catch what the G-man cannot see.

I was different when I was born,

G-man took me; by C-sec I was torn.

Lightning flows around me, but it don't harm me none.

G-man had me programmed – Must obey, get the job done.

Black Vans and Helicopters with their piercing eyes of light.

Black Vans and Helicopters search the dead grounds of the night.

Black Vans and Helicopters with limbs of twenty and the head of one.

Black Vans and Helicopters got me looking back, as on I run.

G-mans got the truth hidden up his sleeve.

But he won't tell it to ya, while he's chasing after me.

Someday death will take me, and it will set me free.

Cause the G-man cannot catch, what the G-man cannot see.

CARMEN SANDIEGO

This poem was inspired by the Saturday morning cartoon show

Carmen SanDiego is a criminal mastermind
who chooses her targets with style and grace;
and dares Zach and me to catch her
by leaving clues to solve the case.

She stole the egg of Russia,
created a diamond Microchip,
She stole the house that OZ built
and captained a ghost pirate ship.

Dressed all in red, from head to toe
she travels back in time.
Though making England of America
was not her greatest crime.

With the temptation, of the greatest game yet,
a cocky young boy, his life he did bet.
And though Lee Jordon she tried to train,
his own ego was his greatest bane.

I'm going to capture Carmen SanDiego
and teach her that crime doesn't pay.
I'm going to capture Carmen
and I'll make her rue the day.

"All I want to do is capture Carmen
so that I can be detective of the year."
I just sat looking at my brother Zach,
who was grinning from ear to ear.

Stakeouts are long and boring
sitting and waiting is the hardest part.
But if Carmen shows up here tonight,
We'll take her away in a Police cart.

This game we play, between her and us
has had many surprising twists and turns.

Yet neither Outer space nor time itself
can take away our desire that burns.
I'm going to capture Carmen,
and today could be the day.
We'll read her rights – slap on the cuffs
and take all her toys away.

For gadgets upon gadgets have helped her pull the crimes.

And maybe without her gadgets she'll finally do the time.

Of the World's Greatest Thief, I must give her due.

For if Carmen ever died, even our chief would miss her too.

GABRIELLE'S DEFENSE

This poem was inspired by Renaissance Pictures' XENA: Warrior Princess

"That's not Xena, not anymore,
refrain from the sword is what she swore.
She won't fight and she won't kill
unless it's for the truth, then she will."

"Xena's army came one day
and took my family all away.
She left me in this world alone
now for her sins she must atone."

"What you want is Xena dead.
But I won't give you Xena's head.
She has changed and done a lot of good.
You won't see that, but you should."

"Xena burned my village to the ground
and left none but children standing 'round.
She laughed her best as the flames rose higher
throwing body upon body into the fire."

"But Xena's never killed a wife or maiden.
She's never killed a babe or the arms it's laid in.
I think their deaths were by another,
by someone who mourns for her own mother."

"Who but Xena could there be so?"
"I think your killer is Callisto."
"But who's Callisto and what's her yearn?"
"Callisto's village Xena burned.
Callisto took the sword t kill Xena,
but it was she who became even meaner.
She killed all who stood fast in her way.
I think it she who took your friends away."

"I will find her, though I may go beyond the river Euphrates!"

"You won't find her unless you go to Hades.
Callisto is paying for her crimes and sin.
So the path of the sword, I beg don't begin.
The sword will only bring you heartache and pain.
Ask my husband Perticus and he'd tell you the same."

"Where is your husband? With him I'll have a word."

"In the Elision Fields, he too died by the sword."

"Your friend Xena doesn't sound so bad."

"She is the best friend I ever had.
Don't get me wrong, she's committed her crimes,
but every day of her life, she does her time.
She's haunted by the ghosts of the dead,
when she lays down to rest her head.

Late at night, you'll hear them moan,
Xena burned my fields and home.
Xena burned my fields and home."

"Come on Gabrielle! It's time to leave."

"Tell me Gabrielle, in her do you believe?"
"I believe in only one thing,
that it is the power of love that makes the world sing."

IN THE GALACTIC SPACE FORCE

In the Galactic Space Force, we sail to the stars.

In the Galactic Space Force, we protect what is ours.

In the Galactic Space Force, we'll be put to the test.

And shine right through like Super Novas, because we are the best.

When I was just a young lad, my father said to me,

"Son, in order to become a real man, you must go to sea."

But the open ocean was not the way for me,

So, I joined the Stellar Navy and twas a woman that set me free.

The navy made of me, a he-man brave and strong,

as I learned to fix our solar sails that help us move along.

There is only one problem – Now- that I can see.

A he-man I am today, but a woman I used to be.

In the Galactic Space Force, we sail to other planets.

In the Galactic Space Force, we'll take anybody's bets.

In the Galactic Space Force, we rock and roll till the dawn,

cause the Galactic Space Force is full of muscle, brains, and fawns.

My mother wanted me to be more lady-like
and she told me "Act you age."
But I was to adventurous
to keep my name from off the page.

So, I signed up for a lifelong mission
and I care not for what I lack

for I'd rather have a Sgt. in my hair,
than my mother upon my back.

We chart the solar system, planets, quasars, and other rocks,
and the closer we get to the speed of light, the slower go our clocks.
Half the crew is in suspended animation – with extra time to sleep;
with temps below sub-zero and baking soda to help them keep.

The Galactic Space Force is the place to be,
cause all our food, rent and clothes are absolutely free.
The Galactic Space Force is universal fun,
so come join us for a cruise to someone else's sun.

PART X
WORK

BORED OUT OF MY MIND

Bored out my mind
   This day is too long.
   Bored out my mind
   is the name of this song.

   Sit and wait
   Write and sleep
   Wonder what
   Tomorrow to eat.

   Bored out my mind
   waning fast
   Bored out my mind
   how long will last.
   Tap my toes
   Twiddle my thumbs
   Stare at the clock
   Will five o'clock come.

Bored out my mind
with a great sigh
Bored out my mind
wishing to fly.

Three O'clock's here and two O'clock's gone
Just two more hours to hang on.
Waiting for five, I want to go home
Staring into space where thoughts roam.

Bored out my mind
this day is too long
Bored out my mind
is the name of this song.

GET ME OUT OF THIS TOWN

Xerox Copying, Left and right
  Answer the phone, may I help you tonight
  Metro is crowded and the buses are jammed
  Kick the dog and refrigerator slam.
  Oh, Get me out of this town.
  cause, I don't want to hang around.

  Boss is in my face
  and Momma's on my back.
  Doc checks my mind
  and tells me I'm a Quack
  Oh, get me out of here
  cause, my heart is heavy and I'm feeling queer.
  Got no money and I haven't a car.
  I want to travel, but so far…
  Oh, get me out of this state

On my life, I want a rebate.
To do what I want and just have fun.
I want to fly a plane and then buy me one.
Oh, get me out of this room.
cause I got to chase away this gloom.

Oh, get me out of this town.
cause, I don't want to hang around.
Oh, get me out of here
cause, my heart is heavy and I'm feeling queer.

Oh, get me out of this state
On my life, I want a rebate.
Oh, get me out of this room.
cause I got to chase away this gloom.

IT'S A QUARTER TILL FIVE

It's a quarter till five, almost the end of the day.
It's a quarter till five, and I'm ready to play.
I want to go home and then to a bar.
I want to go to a movie and then travel far,
Far, far, far away from here.

It's a quarter till five, and I'm ready to leave.
But time's slowing down, that's what I believe.
It's a quarter till five, and I want to go.
Oh, please Lord God, don't let it snow,
Snow, snow, snow outside tonight.

It's a quarter till five, and I'm ready to flee.
But the phone keeps ringing, it just won't let me be.
It's a quarter till five, Oh, time please hurry.

It can rain all it wants, but please no flurries.

It's ten to five, four, three, two, one.
That's it! The day's over and now it's time for fun.

ROCK THE HOSPITAL

EKG and MRI
    Tell me Doctor, will I live or die.
    Mammograms and X-ray bones
    Over the speaker I hear tones,
    Paging Doctor Luke – Paging Doctor Luke.

    Rock the Hospital
    Riding in an Ambulance
    Rock the Hospital
    Back and forth the Nurses prance.

    Rock the Hospital
    Waiting on a gurney -Stat!
    Rock the Hospital
    Got no insurance, throw him back.

    This man's dead, call the morgue!
    This one's bite is from a dog.

Watch her pulse, its fading fast!
This limb's broken, make a cast.

Doctor Ann to O.R. please.
Doctor Robert to the Nursery.
Doctor Jim to the Psycho Ward.
Please have out your ID card.

Rock the Hospital
Nurse, give me another one.
Rock the Hospital
Sniffing gas is so much fun.

Rock the Hospital
Paging Doctor Luke – again.
Rock the Hospital
Pass the sutures- Let's begin.

WHAT A DAY THIS HAS BEEN

What a day, what a day, what a day this has been.

My heart's completely broken and my head's in a spin.

I got up late this morning, I couldn't find the clock.
Didn't eat breakfast, toast was hard as a rock.
With my paper, my dog ran away.
Oh, my god, what a start to my day.

I put soap in and now my clothes are all pink.
I look at my spouse and he's on the brink.
The kids are trouble and always in my hair.
So now my mind is gone, and I don't even care.

What a day, what a day, what a day this has been.

My heart's completely broken and my head's in a spin.

All my bills are overdue, and my house is falling in.

My car's a piece of junk; can't think in all this din.

Hit the stop button and hit replay.
I'd like to get off, or restart the day.
Or better yet lay me in a dirt brown bed.
And put up a sign that says, "Don't wake the dead."

What a day, what a day, what a day this has been.

My heart's completely broken and my head's in a spin.

What happened to the days of a trouble-free youth?

What happened to the days of black and white truth?

What happened to the days when I was happy and free?

Why does my life seem to be

out of my control and too heavy for me?

What a day, what a day, what a day this has been.

My heart's completely broken and my head's in a spin.

WORKING DAYS

The paper one morning said need Asst. Please apply.
   So, I grabbed a resume and I came looking fly.

   He looked me over and asked my name.
   I interviewed and hour before the answer came.
   "Congratulations dear, you got the job.
   You start tomorrow and my name is Bob.

   Now every morning I start at nine,
with so much to copy, I run out of time.
I get coffee and I get the mail,
I'm movin' so fast that I almost fell.
I take calls and I copy, and I eat on the run.
Always too much work, to get it all done.
   The phone rings off the hook as people come and go.

Some appointments come early and some never show.

When it's time to go home, I'm as glad as can be.
Cause workin' ain't no fun, when you're a secretary.
Traffics all around me, but I don't mind.
Cause the guy one car over got eyes bright and kind.

My drive home is nice as can be
cause I ain't got no boss a screamin' at me.
Why in the world must I work for a living?
Taking the money, and bull, and the rest that I'm given.
Who needs to work, I just want to play,
but I can't do that without really good pay.
As bad as work is, it's necessary too,
cause without my work, I'd have nothing to do.

So, I take calls and I copy, and I eat on the run.

"He's not in, she is out, and no the letter's not done."

Someday I'll have a corner office and I'll look upon the sky.

But with my luck, the way that it is, it will be the day…afore I die.

Here lies a lowly secretary whose work was of the highest class.

And what did all that work get her, a nice spot here in the grass.

Here lies a lowly secretary her work now is all done.

She's in heaven now, raisin' hell and having fun.

Other books by Tracy Carol Taylor

60 Christian Traits
The Basics of Christianity
Parody of Parables
The Journey
Small Fry Tales
Toothache at Big Mouth Bend
Cavities of the Caribbean
Your Dental ABCs
Toothtown Football

Available at
www.princeofpages.com